INTIMATE MARRIAGE
S E R I E S

THE GOAL
OF MARRIAGE

Dan B. Allender
and Tremper Longman III

6 STUDIES FOR INDIVIDUALS, COUPLES OR GROUPS

IVP Connect
An imprint of InterVarsity Press
Downers Grove, Illinois

InterVarsity Press
P.O. Box 1400, Downers Grove, IL 60515-1426
World Wide Web: www.ivpress.com
E-mail: mail@ivpress.com

InterVarsity Press® is the book-publishing division of InterVarsity Christian Fellowship/USA®, a student
movement active on campus at hundreds of universities, colleges and schools of nursing in the United States
of America, and a member movement of the International Fellowship of Evangelical Students. For
information about local and regional activities, write Public Relations Dept., InterVarsity Christian
Fellowship/USA, 6400 Schroeder Rd., P.O. Box 7895, Madison, WI 53707-7895, or visit the IVCF website
at <www.intervarsity.org>.

Unless otherwise indicated, all Scripture quotations are taken from the Holy Bible, New Living Translation,
copyright ©1996, 2004. Used by permission of Tyndale House Publishers, Inc., Wheaton, Illinois 60189. All
rights reserved.

Design: Cindy Kiple

Images: JP Fruchet/Getty Images

ISBN-10: 0-8308-2132-5
ISBN-13: 978-0-8308-2132-7

Printed in the United States of America ∞

| P | 19 | 18 | 17 | 16 | 15 | 14 | 13 | 12 | 11 | 10 | 9 | 8 | 7 | 6 | 5 | 4 | 3 | 2 |
| Y | 21 | 20 | 19 | 18 | 17 | 16 | 15 | 14 | 13 | 12 | 11 | 10 | 09 | 08 | 07 | 06 |

CONTENTS

Welcome to Intimate Marriage Bible Studies. 5

1 KNOWING WHO WE ARE AS HUSBAND AND WIFE 9
Genesis 1:26-31; 2:7

2 LEAVING—FROM THE MALE PERSPECTIVE 15
Genesis 2

3 LEAVING—FROM THE FEMALE PERSPECTIVE 21
Psalm 45:10-15

4 WEAVING 25
Ecclesiastes 4:7-12

5 CLEAVING 30
Genesis 2:18-25

6 THE ULTIMATE LOYALTY 34
Psalm 127

Leader's Notes 39

113666

WELCOME TO
INTIMATE MARRIAGE
BIBLE STUDIES

THE GOAL OF MARRIAGE

Why do people get married? The answers may vary, but most would probably say that they have fallen in love and want to be with that person permanently. Or perhaps they would mention their desire for security, partnership, sexual intimacy or children.

This study asks about the *biblical* goal of marriage. The book of Genesis tells us that God created the institution of marriage in the Garden of Eden. It also tells us that he established a pattern for that marriage when he stated that a man leave his parents, weave a relationship with his wife and cleave to her in sexual union. The following six studies look at passages from Genesis as well as elsewhere to explore the significance of these three actions for a good marriage. The last study will point out that the relationship between a husband and a wife is only as strong as their individual and joint relationship with the God who created marriage.

TAKING MARRIAGE SERIOUSLY

Most of us want to have a good marriage. Those who don't have a good relationship yearn for a better one, and those who have a good one want even more intimacy.

We want to know our spouse and be known by them. We want to be loved and to love. In short, we want the type of marriage desired by God from the beginning when he created the institution of marriage and defined it as involving leaving parents, weaving a life of intimacy together and cleaving in sexual bliss.

These studies delve into the wisdom of the Bible in order to learn what it takes to have not just a "good" marriage but one that enjoys the relational richness that God intended for a husband and a wife. This divinely instituted type of marriage is one that will

- Bring a husband and wife closer together
- Understand that marriage is one's primary loyalty to other human beings
- Be characterized by a growing love and knowledge of one another
- Be an arena of spiritual growth
- Allow for the healthy exposure of sin through the offer of forgiveness
- Be a crucible for showing grace
- Reflect God's love for his people
- Enjoy God's gift of sexual intimacy
- Share life's joys and troubles
- Have a part in transforming us from sinners to saints
- Bring out each other's glory as divine image bearers

And so much more! The Bible provides a wealth of insight, and these studies hope to tap its riches and bring them to bear on our marriage relationships.

USING THE STUDIES

These studies can be used in a variety of contexts—individual de-
votional life, by a couple together or by a small group—or in a
combination of these settings. Each study includes the following
components.

Open. Several quotes at the beginning give a sense of what
married people say about the topic at hand. These are followed
by a question that can be used for discussion. If you are using
the DVD, you may want to skip this and go straight to the opening clip.

DVD Reflection. For each session we have an opening thought
from Dan Allender, at times accompanied by an excerpt from our
interviews with married couples, to get you thinking about the
topic at hand. This material will provide fresh and engaging
openers for a small group as well as interesting discussion points
for couples studying together. You will find a question here to discuss after you watch the DVD clip.

Study. One or more key Bible texts are included in the guide
for convenience. We have chosen the New Living Translation,
but you may use any version of Scripture you like. The questions in this section will take you through the key aspects of the
passage and help you apply them to your marriage. Sprinkled
throughout the study, you will also find commentary to enrich
your experience.

For the Couple. Here's an opportunity to make an application
and commitment, which is specific to your marriage.

Bonus. These are further ideas for study on your own. Or if you are studying with a group, take time to do the bonus item with your spouse during the week.

We hope that these studies enrich your marriage. We encourage you to be brutally honest with yourself and tactfully honest with your spouse. If you are willing to be honest with yourself and with the Scripture, then God will do great things for your marriage. That is our prayer.

KNOWING WHO WE ARE
AS HUSBAND AND WIFE

"People are ugly and evil. I just can't trust anyone."

"I believe in the fundamental goodness of my fellow human beings."

▶ OPEN

We hear blanket statements like these all the time. We may even make them ourselves from time to time. In reality, though, people can be annoying or just bland, dangerous, threatening and morally ugly, yet they can occasionally be nice and helpful, and even heroic. How do you view your fellow human beings?

Go further: how do you think of yourself and your spouse?

▶ DVD REFLECTION

What intrigues you about how Dan Allender describes the goal of marriage? What troubles or surprises you?

▶ STUDY

Have you ever reflected on the implications of our origins in the Garden? How might that affect our attitudes and behavior toward other people and particularly toward our spouse? The account of our creation in the first two chapters of Genesis gives us a basis to explore these crucial questions.

Genesis contains stories of beginnings, told not for simply intellectual interest but because a knowledge of our origins is crucial for our self-understanding. In Genesis we go back to our deepest roots, and we come back wiser.

To understand marriage, we need to come to grips first of all with who we are as humans. Who are we, and how do we fit into God's vast creation? In this study we will explore who we are as human beings created by God. In a later study we will explore the significance of the difference in the creation of Adam (male) and Eve (female).

IN THE BEGINNING

The book of Genesis is a book of "beginnings" or "origins." Indeed that is precisely what the name Genesis means when translated from the Greek, and the Hebrew name of the book comes from the first phrase, bereshit, "in the beginning."

Read Genesis 1:26-31.

²⁶Then God said, "Let us make human beings in our image, to be like ourselves. They will reign over the fish in the sea, the birds in the sky, the livestock, all the wild animals on the earth, and the small animals that scurry along the ground."

²⁷So God created human beings in his own image.

In the image of God he created them;

male and female he created them.

²⁸Then God blessed them and said, "Be fruitful and multiply. Fill the earth and govern it. Reign over the fish in the sea, the birds in the sky, and all the animals that scurry along the ground."

²⁹Then God said, "Look! I have given you every seed-bearing plant throughout the earth and all the fruit trees for your food. ³⁰And I have given every green plant as food for all the wild animals, the birds in the sky, and the small animals that scurry along the ground—everything that has life." And that is what happened.

³¹Then God looked over all he had made, and he saw that it was very good!

And evening passed and morning came, marking the sixth day.

Read Genesis 2:7.

⁷Then the LORD God formed the man from the dust of the ground. He breathed the breath of life into the man's nostrils, and the man became a living person.

1. How does God respond to the great array of his creation (1:31)?

2. What is significant about God's creating Adam on the sixth day of creation?

3. God says that humans (both male and female; 1:27) are created
   in his image. Read the sidebar on what it means that we are created in the image of God. How does this affect how you see
   yourself?

▼

IMAGE OF GOD

*Nothing sounds more uplifting than the statement that we are cre-
ated in the image of God. Though that's a good thing, what exactly
does it mean?*

*Some people suggest that the image must point to something
unique in human beings, since animals are never said to be created
in God's image. This would mean that a human trait like reason or
the ability to communicate through language marks the image of
God in a person.*

*However, a better route to an answer begins when we ask what
an image meant in its Old Testament context. How would an ancient
Israelite have heard the word image?*

*Kings in the ancient Near East would have images or statues of
themselves set up all around their kingdom. These statues repre-
sented the king and reflected his glory and power. Thus "image of
God" in Genesis 1:27 indicates that human beings reflect God's
glory and represent his presence on earth. Image-bearers reflect the
divine glory. The glory is reflected as the moon reflects the light of
the sun. When we look into the face of another human being, we
see the face of God.*

4. What does being made in God's image mean for the relationship between God and his human creatures?

5. What does it mean that men and women "rule over" the other creatures God has made?

6. In Genesis 2:7 we learn that God created the first person from the dust of the ground and the breath of God. What implication does that have for how humans relate to God and God's other creatures?

7. Your spouse is created in the image of God. How should this biblical truth influence your relationship? (Reflect on both attitude and behavior.)

8. What can make it difficult to see God's image reflected in the life of another person?

▶ FOR THE COUPLE

Reflect on your spouse as created in God's image. How does that perception change your attitude and behavior toward your spouse?

What obstacles keep you from seeing him or her as a divine image-bearer?

▶ BONUS

Psalm 8 reflects on the place of human beings in God's creation. Read this psalm. As you meditate on it, make it specific. Think of the language as describing you and your spouse.

▼

"A LITTLE LOWER THAN . . ."

Some popular versions translate Psalm 8:5 "For you made us only a little lower than heavenly beings." However, the Hebrew clearly supports the New Living Translation (and most other versions), which takes the comparison as between humans and God, not angels.

What does the psalm mean when it says that God made humans (you and your spouse) "only a little lower than God" (v. 5)?

In the same verse, what does it mean to be crowned with glory and honor?

Is your attitude and behavior toward your spouse shaped by viewing him or her as "crowned with glory and honor"? Why or why not?

LEAVING—FROM THE MALE PERSPECTIVE

"Your father is always looking over my shoulder. I know he loves you as his little girl, but it makes me feel like a three-year-old!"

"I know your father was handy around the house, but I'm not. Can't we just pay someone to fix it?"

▶ OPEN

How is marriage different from any other relationship you have?

And what impact, if any, should marriage have on previous relationships with, say, friends and parents?

▶ DVD REFLECTION

What are the risks for a man in leaving his parents behind?

▶ STUDY

Read Genesis 2.

So the creation of the heavens and the earth and everything in them was completed. ²On the seventh day, God had finished his work of creation, so he rested from all his work. ³And God blessed the seventh day and declared it holy, because it was the day when he rested from all his work of creation.

⁴This is the account of the creation of the heavens and the earth. When the LORD God made the earth and the heavens, ⁵neither wild plants nor grains were growing on the earth. The LORD God had not yet sent rain to water the earth, and there were no people to cultivate the soil. ⁶Instead, springs came up from the ground and watered all the land. ⁷Then the LORD God formed the man from the dust of the ground. He breathed the breath of life into the man's nostrils, and the man became a living person.

⁸Then the LORD God planted a garden in Eden in the east, and there he placed the man he had made. ⁹The LORD God made all sorts of trees grow up from the ground—trees that were beautiful and produced delicious fruit. In the middle of the garden he placed the tree of life and the tree of the knowledge of good and evil.

¹⁰A river watered the garden and then flowed out of Eden and divided into four branches. ¹¹The first branch, called the Pishon, flowed around the entire land of Havilah, where gold is found. ¹²The gold of that land is exceptionally pure; aromatic resin and onyx stone are also found there. ¹³The second branch, called Gihon, flowed around the entire land of Cush. ¹⁴The third branch, called the Tigris, flowed east of the land of Asshur. The fourth branch is called the Euphrates.

¹⁵The LORD God placed the man in the Garden of Eden to tend and watch over it. ¹⁶But the LORD God warned him, "You may freely eat the fruit of every tree in the garden—¹⁷except the tree of the knowledge of good and evil. If you eat its fruit, you are sure to die."

[18]Then the LORD God said, "It is not good for the man to be alone. I will make a helper who is just right for him." [19]So the LORD God formed from the ground all the wild animals and all the birds of the sky. He brought them to the man to see what he would call them, and the man chose a name for each one. [20]He gave names to all the livestock, all the birds of the sky, and all the wild animals. But still there was no helper just right for him.

[21]So the LORD God caused the man to fall into a deep sleep. While the man slept, the LORD God took out one of the man's ribs and closed up the opening. [22]Then the LORD God made a woman from the rib, and he brought her to the man.

[23]"At last!" the man exclaimed.

"This one is bone from my bone,
    and flesh from my flesh!
She will be called 'woman,'
    because she was taken from 'man.' "

[24]This explains why a man leaves his father and mother and is joined to his wife, and the two are united into one.

[25]Now the man and his wife were both naked, but they felt no shame.

1. Notice Adam's first task (vv. 19-20). What does it suggest about the role of human beings made in God's image?

2. What lack does God recognize in Adam, in the midst of an abundant creation?

What events or situations in your life have made you aware of your need for others?

WHY POETRY?

Genesis 2:23-25 is the first poem in the Bible. Poetry is the language of song. Adam breaks out into a joyous song when he first encounters his beloved Eve. Later in the Bible we encounter the Song of Songs, a whole book of song-poems celebrating marital love.

3. Why is Adam excited when he encounters the woman?

What does this tell us about the purpose of marriage?

"WOMAN" FROM "MAN"

"She will be called 'woman,' because she was taken from 'man' "
(Gen 2:23). The English wordplay reflects well the Hebrew, where
the word for "woman" (ishsha) is related to the word for "man" (ish).
Again, even the words indicate the intimate connection between the
man and the woman.

4. What does verse 23 suggest about the nature of the relationship between Adam and Eve, a husband and a wife?

5. What does it mean for a man to leave his parents in order to be united to his wife? (Does it necessarily involve a physical separation?)

6. List some of the difficulties that can keep men from truly leaving their parents when they get married.

7. How does leaving parents help a new couple grow closer to each other?

How does not leaving hinder intimacy?

8. What are some other previous attachments, which could hinder intimacy, that are particularly difficult for men to leave?

▶ FOR THE COUPLE

Spend some time reflecting on past commitments that keep you from fully embracing your spouse. Make a list of loyalties from your past that you suspect your spouse would say you are reluctant to break. What would keep you from giving up these past commitments? If you can discuss this without accusation and with a spirit of honesty and prayer, then share your separate lists.

▶ BONUS

Genesis 2 pictures marriage as a remedy for loneliness. Reflect on these questions.

Are single people incomplete?

Are married couples never lonely?

3

LEAVING—FROM THE FEMALE PERSPECTIVE

"Why do you always want me to cook the chicken your mom's way?"

"Can we stay at home and have our own Christmas celebration this year?"

▶ OPEN

The first step in the establishment of a marriage, "leaving," is the establishment of a new primary loyalty. In Genesis 2:24 a man is called to leave his parents to join in a new relationship with a wife. But the woman must leave as well. What do you think would be some of the particular issues or difficulties for the woman in leaving?

▶ DVD REFLECTION

What are the rewards for a woman in leaving her parents behind?

▶ STUDY

Now we turn to Psalm 45 in order to explore not just the importance of leaving for the couple but also, in particular, for the woman. What does it mean for a woman to leave her parents?

Read Psalm 45:10-15.

[10]Listen to me, O royal daughter; take to heart what I say.

Forget your people and your family far away.

[11]For your royal husband delights in your beauty;

honor him, for he is your lord.

[12]The princess of Tyre will shower you with gifts.

The wealthy will beg your favor.

[13]The bride, a princess, looks glorious

in her golden gown.

[14]In her beautiful robes, she is led to the king,

accompanied by her bridesmaids.

[15]What a joyful and enthusiastic procession

as they enter the king's palace!

1. The princess has come from far away to marry the king. What struggles do you think she had to "forget" her father's house (v. 10)?

2. What do you think the singers mean when they tell her to "forget" her father's house?

THE BACKGROUND OF PSALM 45

Psalm 45 is unique among the poems in the book of Psalms. It is a royal wedding song, celebrating the union of one of Israel's kings to a woman from Tyre. Many historical questions remain, especially, who is the couple that inspired this uplifting psalm? However, answering such questions is relatively unimportant for the interpretation and application of the psalm today. After all, though inspired by specific historical events, the psalms speak to our own lives. Though we are not royalty, the grandeur of the Psalm 45 wedding tells us something about the importance of the institution of marriage, and a number of the principles expressed in the poem are still relevant. One of the latter has to do with our present subject: the importance of leaving previous commitments as one enters into a new relationship.

3. Do you think the request is fair?

4. What do you think it means for the "royal daughter" to honor her husband (v. 11)?

5. How would a wife honor her husband today?

6. Do you think this Scripture teaches that honor goes one way (only wife to a husband)? Explain.

7. Is leaving one's parents in favor of loyalty to your spouse an action you can carry out in a moment of decision and be done with? Why or why not?

▶ FOR THE COUPLE

Talk about any areas of your marriage where you still struggle with issues of leaving.

▶ BONUS

What role do parents have in the leaving process? How can a newly married couple and their parents cooperate in this rather than being at odds?

4

WEAVING

"I feel secure with her. I trust her."

"He is my rock of Gibraltar. I can count on him."

"We look forward to growing old together."

▶ OPEN

Genesis 2:24 says that a man leaves his parents in order to be joined to his wife. For this to work, we assume that the woman too is to leave her parents and join her husband (see also Psalm 45). Thus in marriage two lives are woven together.

In both ancient Israel and modern society, marriage is a relationship established and governed by law. So this joining involves a legal dimension. A husband can't wake up one morning and decide to have nothing to do with his wife, or vice versa. There would be legal ramifications. But joining involves more than a legal connection. Much, much more than law unites a husband and a wife. What is one thing that has helped you to weave your lives together?

▶ DVD REFLECTION

What does it mean for a married couple to weave their two lives into one?

▶ STUDY

The text we are going to read in Ecclesiastes does not speak specifically of marriage, but it celebrates the benefits of a companion. Marriage is the most intimate type of relationship, and therefore we can learn about marriage from studying what Scripture says about relationships in general.

Read Ecclesiastes 4:7-12.

⁷I observed yet another example of something meaningless under the sun. ⁸This is the case of a man who is all alone, without a child or a brother, yet who works hard to gain as much wealth as he can. But then he asks himself, "Who am I working for? Why am I giving up so much pleasure now?" It is all so meaningless and depressing.

⁹Two people are better off than one, for they can help each other succeed. ¹⁰If one person falls, the other can reach out and help. But someone who falls alone is in real trouble. ¹¹Likewise, two people lying close together can keep each other warm. But how can one be warm alone? ¹²A person standing alone can be attacked and defeated, but two can stand back-to-back and conquer. Three are even better, for a triple-braided cord is not easily broken.

1. Reread Genesis 2:23-25 (p. 17), and reflect again on the institution of marriage as established and described here. In what ways do a woman and a man join (weave) their lives together in marriage?

2. According to Ecclesiastes 4:7-12, what advantages are there to entering into an interdependent relationship with another?

3. While Ecclesiastes 4:7-12 refers to friendship, how do the advantages of friendship also apply to a marriage relationship?

THE TRIPLE-BRAIDED CORD

Ecclesiastes 4:12 speaks of the triple-braided cord: three is even better than one. This verse is often misunderstood to refer to the Trinity, or to a person, their friend and God, although this simple image is found in at least one other ancient extrabiblical text (Gilgamesh and the Land of the Living). The argument of the Ecclesiastes passage up to this point is that having a friend has tremendous advantages—two is better than one). The concluding verse makes the point that if having one friend is good, having more than one is even better.

4. What are some concrete steps a married couple can take to weave their lives together?

5. What kinds of things can hinder two people from joining their lives together?

How can these obstacles be overcome?

NEGOTIATION AND COMPROMISE

Is it okay to argue and wrangle to convince your spouse of your perspective? Is it honorable to attempt to persuade your spouse of your opinion? Yes, absolutely. Persuasion is a form of rhetoric that attempts to win the heart and action of another by an appeal to emotion, wisdom and vision. What is not honorable is pressure, guilt or coercion.

When you seek to persuade your spouse, it's best to announce your desire to persuade and then launch into a time-limited "presentation" with plenty of opportunity for critique and eventual compromise. The goal must never be to gain your will alone. The true goal of persuasion is the greater good of creating together a plan that includes both perspectives.

6. Does being joined together require that a husband and a wife give up their individuality altogether? Explain your response.

7. How should a couple negotiate their union and their individuality? (Is it appropriate to talk about individual rights in a marriage?)

8. An important part of weaving is how you share your time together. How can a couple tell when a desire to preserve "space" from a spouse is right or wrong?

▶ FOR THE COUPLE

Examine your schedules to see how often you have time together to actually share your lives. What are the obstacles to creating time together?

How can these obstacles be overcome?

Do you have what you both consider to be a healthy balance of shared and individual interests and activities?

Where do you find it easy to weave your lives together, and where is it difficult?

▶ BONUS

Read 1 Corinthians 13:4-8. In light of this text, describe love using your own words. How does the cultivation of this type of love enhance the possibility of weaving two lives into one?

5

CLEAVING

"I don't have words to express the intense, deep pleasure of making love with my husband."

"Our sex life has improved with each year of marriage."

▶ OPEN

Genesis 2, which has established marriage, culminates with the sexual union of a man and a woman. Why would the Bible point to sexual relations as the end point of marriage?

▶ DVD REFLECTION

Why is sex preceded by leaving and weaving?

▶ STUDY

Genesis 2 provides us with a theological foundation for sex in marriage, and thus in this study we return to the second half of that chapter.

Read Genesis 2:18-25.

[18]Then the LORD God said, "It is not good for the man to be alone. I will make a helper who is just right for him." [19]So the LORD God formed from the ground all the wild animals and all the birds of the sky. He brought them to the man to see what he would call them, and the man chose a name for each one. [20]He gave names to all the livestock, all the birds of the sky, and all the wild animals. But still there was no helper just right for him.

[21]So the LORD God caused the man to fall into a deep sleep. While the man slept, the LORD God took out one of the man's ribs and closed up the opening. [22]Then the LORD God made a woman from the rib, and he brought her to the man.

[23]"At last!" the man exclaimed.

"This one is bone from my bone,
    and flesh from my flesh!
She will be called 'woman,'
    because she was taken from 'man.' "

[24]This explains why a man leaves his father and mother and is joined to his wife, and the two are united into one.

[25]Now the man and his wife were both naked, but they felt no shame.

1. Why do you think God parades all the animals in front of Adam in the quest for a partner suitable for him?

2. What significance do you see in Eve's being created from the very body of Adam?

3. Notice that children are not mentioned in this passage, not even in the statement about the two becoming "one flesh." Explore possible reasons for this.

4. How do Adam and Eve respond to each other's nakedness?

What permits this response?

5. What is beautiful about marital sexual intercourse?

6. Cleaving follows leaving and weaving. Why is it the third and climactic action in the establishment of marriage? Why is it the end point?

7. Genesis 2:18 cites loneliness as the problem God solves by creating marriage. How does sexual intimacy answer the loneliness problem?

▶ FOR THE COUPLE

In what ways do you and your spouse experience one-flesh intimacy?

What can you do to increase that intimacy?

Describe to each other times when you felt the deepest intimacy with each other.

▶ BONUS

Why is sex such a powerful force in our lives?

THE ULTIMATE
LOYALTY

"There is only one person more important to me than my spouse—God himself."

"Before we became Christians, our marriage did not have a foundation."

▶ OPEN

Fundamental to marriage is the creation of a new primary loyalty. A husband must relate to his wife and a wife to her husband in a unique way. The Bible makes clear, however, that another relationship is even more fundamental than marriage. That relationship, of course, is with God.

What are some ways your relationship with God intersects with your marriage relationship?

▶ DVD REFLECTION

What is the greatest priority of your marriage?

▶ STUDY

Read Psalm 127.

A song for pilgrims ascending to Jerusalem. A psalm of Solomon.

¹Unless the LORD builds a house,
　　the work of the builders is wasted.
Unless the LORD protects a city,
　　guarding it with sentries will do no good.
²It is useless for you to work so hard
　　from early morning until late at night,
anxiously working for food to eat;
　　for God gives rest to his loved ones.

³Children are a gift from the LORD;
　　they are a reward from him.
⁴Children born to a young man
　　are like arrows in a warrior's hands.
⁵How joyful is the man whose quiver is full of them!
　　He will not be put to shame when he confronts his accusers
　　　　at the city gates.

A SONG FOR THE ASCENT TO JERUSALEM

A title attached to Psalm 127 (and all the psalms from 120 to 134) is "A Song of Ascent." "To Jerusalem," added in the New Living Translation, is a helpful interpretive addition. These songs were sung by religious pilgrims as they journeyed to Jerusalem from surrounding towns and villages to worship at the temple during one of Israel's great annual religious festivals.

1. How can the Lord "build a house"?

    In what ways can you relate to this from your own experience?

2. What does the psalmist mean when he says that it is useless to
   work very hard?

    How does this apply to marriage and family life?

3. What place should God play in a marriage relationship?

4. What particular sin is committed when a husband or a wife makes their spouse more important than God?

5. What, in particular, happens to a wife if her husband puts her first, or to a husband if his wife puts him first?

6. Putting one's spouse first isn't the only way to threaten a strong foundation of marriage. What other things can get in the way and become idols?

7. How does a couple put God first in their relationship?

▶ **FOR THE COUPLE**

Reflect together on your relationship with God. What do you have to be thankful for?

In what ways can you together deepen your relationship with God?

▶ **BONUS**

Read Matthew 7:24-29. How does Jesus' teaching here relate to Psalm 127?

How does this teaching relate to marriage?

Then read 2 Corinthians 6:14-18. Does this teaching have anything to do with marriage? If so, how?

What happens if a Christian is already in a committed relationship with an unbeliever?

LEADER'S NOTES

My grace is sufficient for you.

2 CORINTHIANS 12:9 NIV

Leading a Bible discussion can be an enjoyable and rewarding experience. But it can also be *scary*—especially if you've never done it before. If this is your feeling, you're in good company. When God asked Moses to lead the Israelites out of Egypt, he replied, "O Lord, please send someone else to do it" (Ex 4:13 NIV). It was the same with Solomon, Jeremiah and Timothy, but God helped these people in spite of their weaknesses, and he will help you as well.

You don't need to be an expert on the Bible or a trained teacher to lead a Bible discussion. The idea behind these inductive studies is that the leader guides group members to discover for themselves what the Bible has to say. This method of learning will allow group members to remember much more of what is said than a lecture would.

These studies are designed to be led easily. As a matter of fact, the flow of questions through the passage from observation to interpretation to application is so natural that you may feel that the studies lead themselves. This study guide is also flexible. You can use it with a variety of groups—student, professional, neighborhood or church groups. Each study takes forty-five to sixty minutes in a group setting.

There are some important facts to know about group dynamics and encouraging discussion. The suggestions listed below should enable you to effectively and enjoyably fulfill your role as leader.

PREPARING FOR THE STUDY

1. Ask God to help you understand and apply the passage in your own life. Unless this happens, you will not be prepared to lead others. Pray too for the various members of the group. Ask God to open your hearts to the message of his Word and motivate you to action.

2. Read the introduction to the entire guide to get an overview of the entire book and the issues which will be explored.

3. As you begin each study, read and reread the assigned Bible passage to familiarize yourself with it.

4. This study guide is based on the New Living Translation of the Bible. It will help you and the group if you use this translation as the basis for your study and discussion.

5. Carefully work through each question in the study. Spend time in meditation and reflection as you consider how to respond.

6. Write your thoughts and responses in the space provided in the study guide. This will help you to express your understanding of the passage clearly.

7. It might help to have a Bible dictionary handy. Use it to look up any unfamiliar words, names or places. (For additional help on how to study a passage, see chapter five of *How to Lead a LifeGuide Bible Study,* InterVarsity Press.)

8. Consider how you can apply the Scripture to your life. Remember that the group will follow your lead in responding to the studies. They will not go any deeper than you do.

9. Once you have finished your own study of the passage, familiarize yourself with the leader's notes for the study you are leading. These are designed to help you in several ways. First, they tell you the purpose the study guide author had in mind when writing the study. Take time to think through how the study questions work together to accomplish that purpose. Second, the notes provide you with additional background information or suggestions on group dynamics for various questions. This information can be useful when people have difficulty understanding or answering a question. Third, the leader's notes can alert you to potential problems you may encounter during the study.

10. If you wish to remind yourself of anything mentioned in the leader's notes, make a note to yourself below that question in the study.

LEADING THE STUDY

1. Begin the study on time. Open with prayer, asking God to help the group to understand and apply the passage.

2. Be sure that everyone in your group has a study guide. Encourage the group to prepare beforehand for each discussion by reading the introduction to the guide and by working through the questions in the study.

3. At the beginning of your first time together, explain that these studies are meant to be discussions, not lectures. Encourage the members of the group to participate. However, do not put pressure on those who may be hesitant to speak during the first few sessions. You may want to suggest the following guidelines to your group.

- Stick to the topic being discussed.

- Your responses should be based on the verses that are the focus of the discussion and not on outside authorities such as commentaries or speakers.

- Anything said in the group is considered confidential and will not be discussed outside the group unless specific permission is given to do so.

- Listen attentively to each other and provide time for each person present to talk.

- Pray for each other.

4. Play the DVD clip from the *Intimate Marriage DVD* and use the DVD reflection question to kick off group discussion. You can move directly from there to the beginning of the study section. Or, if you wish, you can also have a group member read the introduction aloud and then you can discuss the question in the "Open" section. If you do not have the DVD, then be sure to kick off the discussion with the question in the "Open" section.

   The "Open" question and the DVD clip are meant to be used before the passage is read. They introduce the theme of the study and encourage members to begin to open up. Encourage as many members as possible to participate, and be ready to get the discussion going with your own response.

This section is designed to reveal where your thoughts or feelings need to be transformed by Scripture. That is why it is especially important not to read the passage before the discussion question is asked. The passage will tend to color the honest reactions people would otherwise give because they are, of course, supposed to think the way the Bible does.

5. Have a group member (or members if the passage is long) read aloud the passage to be studied. Then give people several minutes to read the passage again silently so that they can take it all in.

6. Question 1 will generally be an overview question designed to briefly survey the passage. Encourage the group to look at the whole passage, but try to avoid getting sidetracked by questions or issues that will be addressed later in the study.

7. As you ask the questions, keep in mind that they are designed to be used just as they are written. You may simply read them aloud. Or you may prefer to express them in your own words.

There may be times when it is appropriate to deviate from the study guide. For example, a question may have already been answered. If so, move on to the next question. Or someone may raise an important question not covered in the guide. Take time to discuss it, but try to keep the group from going off on tangents.

8. The sidebars contain further background information on the texts in the study. If they are relevant to the course of your dis-

cussion, you may want to read them aloud. However, to keep the discussion moving, you may want to omit them and allow group members to read them on their own.

9. Avoid answering your own questions. If necessary, repeat or rephrase them until they are clearly understood. Or point out something you read in the leader's notes to clarify the context or meaning. An eager group quickly becomes passive and silent if they think the leader will do most of the talking.

10. Don't be afraid of silence. People may need time to think about the question before formulating their answers.

11. Don't be content with just one answer. Ask, "What do the rest of you think?" or "Anything else?" until several people have given answers to the question.

12. Acknowledge all contributions. Try to be affirming whenever possible. Never reject an answer. If it is clearly off-base, ask, "Which verse led you to that conclusion?" or again, "What do the rest of you think?"

13. Don't expect every answer to be addressed to you, even though this will probably happen at first. As group members become more at ease, they will begin to truly interact with each other. This is one sign of healthy discussion.

14. Don't be afraid of controversy. It can be very stimulating. If you don't resolve an issue completely, don't be frustrated. Move on and keep it in mind for later. A subsequent study may solve the problem.

15. Periodically summarize what the group has said about the

passage. This helps to draw together the various ideas mentioned and gives continuity to the study. But don't preach.

16. At the end of the Bible discussion, give couples an opportunity to discuss the "For the Couple" section and make the application personal. It's important to include this in your group time so that couples don't neglect discussing this material. Of course, sometimes couples may need to discuss the topic long beyond the five minutes of group time allotted, but you can help them get started in the meeting.

17. Encourage group members to work on the "Bonus" section between meetings as a couple or on their own. Give an opportunity during the session for people to talk about what they are learning.

18. End on time.

Many more suggestions and helps on leading a couples group are found in the *Intimate Marriage Leader's Guide*.

COMPONENTS OF SMALL GROUPS

A healthy small group should do more than study the Bible. There are four components to consider as you structure your time together.

Nurture. Small groups help us to grow in our knowledge and love of God. Bible study is the key to making this happen and is the foundation of your small group.

Community. Small groups are a great place to develop deep friendships with other Christians. Allow time for informal interaction before and after each study. Plan activities and games that will help you get to know each other. Spend time having fun to-gether—going on a picnic or cooking dinner together.

Worship and prayer. Your study will be enhanced by spending time praising God together in prayer or song. Pray for each other's needs—and keep track of how God is answering prayer in your group. Ask God to help you to apply what you are learn-ing in your study.

Outreach. Reaching out to others can be a practical way of ap-plying what you are learning, and it will keep your group from becoming self-focused. Host a series of evangelistic discussions for your friends or neighbors. Clean up the yard of an elderly friend. Serve at a soup kitchen together, or spend a day working on a Habitat house.

Many more suggestions and helps in each of these areas are found in *Small Group Idea Book.* Information on building a small group can be found in *The Big Book on Small Groups* (both from InterVarsity Press). Reading through one of these books would be worth your time.

STUDY NOTES

Study 1. Knowing Who We Are as Husband and Wife. Genesis 1:26-31; 2:7.

Purpose: To gain appreciation for how our spouse is made in the image of God and reflects his glory.

Question 1. When God finished creating, he looked at his cre-ation and pronounced that it was excellent.

Question 2. The fact that humans are created last on the sixth day indicates that the previous creation was shaped in preparation for their appearance. In other words, human beings are the climax of creation. The first three days create realms, while the second three days fill each of those realms with inhabitants in turn, so day four fills day one, day five fills day two, and day six fills day three:

Day One	**Day Two**	**Day Three**
light/darkness	sky/water	land

Day Four	**Day Five**	**Day Six**
sun, moon, stars	birds, fish	animals, humans

The climactic creation of human beings does not mean that they have the right to exploit the creation, but it does mean that human beings are the most important creatures in God's vast creation.

Question 3. It means human beings reflect God's glory. See sidebar "Image of God."

Question 4. A very close and intimate relationship exists between God and his image-bearers. They reflect his glory in the broader creation.

Question 5. Human beings are the kings and queens of creation. They reflect their divine Father's heavenly kingship on earth. Humans are responsible for the well-being of creation and the proper use of its resources.

Question 6. The description of the creation of Adam from dust and divine breath shows the complex nature of human relationship to God and the rest of creation. The dust shows that we are creatures, but the animating breath of God shows that we have a special relationship with our Creator.

Genesis 1 was not written to counter modern scientific approaches to the question of human origins, but rather to rival other ancient Near Eastern accounts. With this background, it is striking to note that two creation stories from Mesopotamia (the *Enuma Elish* and *Atrahasis*) also describe the first humans as created from two elements. As in the Genesis account, one of the elements is from the ground (clay), while the other is from the gods. However, the latter is nothing as noble as the breath of God. Rather, one tradition says that the clay was mixed with the spit of the gods, while the other refers to the blood of an executed demon god.

The Mesopotamian myths and the biblical account offer very different perspectives on human beings and their relationship to the divine realm. In the biblical account humans are the apex of creation and in intimate relationship with their Creator. But in the Mesopotamian account they are created to serve the gods in menial tasks and to provide them with food through their sacrifices.

Question 7. This question asks the group to reflect on what it means that one's wife or husband reflects the glory of God, that to look into their face is to see the face of God. Of course this does not mean that humans are divine themselves, but in some way they reflect God's character.

Question 8. Human beings could reflect God's glory in a way that would be easy to see. However, between our creation and the present time stands the Fall and the introduction of sin (Gen 3), which has distorted our reflection of the glory of God. The effects of sin on the image of God and our relationship with one another will be considered in a number of later studies.

Bonus, question 1. It is bold language, but taking it at face value as we should, it tells us that human beings carry great dignity and worth. As our study of Genesis 1—2 indicated, there is nothing quite so precious in God's creation as human beings. As we interact with our spouse, do we realize that we are dealing with a creature who is "only a little lower than God"?

Bonus, question 2. Do you think of your spouse as a fellow monarch? As joint rulers in creation, neither partner gives menial service to the other. The imagery of being rulers serves to evoke respect and awe toward other human beings, including our spouse.

Bonus question 3. Sin is ugly and mars the reflection of God's glory in us and our spouses. Specifically, you may want to consider the following questions:

- Where do you find it hard to trust your spouse?
- What topics are hard to talk about?
- What are the communication issues that make it hard to hope?
- What keeps intimacy from growing in your relationship?
- How can sex become an obstacle to intimacy?

Study 2. Leaving—from the Male Perspective. Genesis 2.

Purpose: To impress on the husband the importance of forming a new primary loyalty with his wife.

Question 1. Here the first human being is given an image-of-God task: to tend and watch the land as God's representative.

Question 2. Adam is lonely, and God recognizes the need for him to have a companion. One purpose of marriage, therefore, seems to be to fill a legitimate need for human companionship.

The Hebrew word translated "helper" is *ezer*. This term does not indicate subservience of any kind. After all, even God is called an *ezer* of Israel in a place like Psalm 46:1. Thus the woman is not pictured as a sort of gofer or assistant who can do the man's menial tasks, but as a strong and much-needed partner and ally.

Question 3. Adam is excited because he recognizes that Eve is the one who will meet his longings. Note that what he recognizes in her is likeness rather than opposition. Instead of crying out, "She is gentle where I am tough! She is Venus, I am Mars!" he speaks lyrically of their sharing the same bone and flesh.

Question 4. Marriage is an intensely intimate relationship. The language used ("my own flesh and bone") and the method of Eve's creation (from Adam's side) make it clear that the union of a man and a woman is a reuniting of an original unity.

Some theologians have proposed that the first human being's need for a counterpart to form a "two yet one" relationship points to a dimension of the image of God. In their interdependence and mutual delight, the first couple are a reflection of the Trinity.

Question 5. There is no relationship as intimate as marriage, and no other relationship is mutually exclusive. But old patterns are hard to break. If a husband or a wife is constantly appealing to parents for advice or help over that of the spouse, the new marriage relationship will not have space to mature.

By highlighting the fact that the husband must leave his father, Scripture is challenging the way things were and still are usually done in most traditional societies around the world. The bride goes to live with her husband's family, and often she is seen as property being transferred from one male-headed household to another. In her new home she can be subject to abuse, since (1) she is physically weaker, (2) her husband is considered to have authority over her, (3) she may be treated as a servant under the domination of her mother-in-law, and (4) she is away from members of her own family who would stand up for her. Bride burnings in India are the most egregious examples of how a man's failure to leave his family of origin can lead to tragedy. Even in ancient Israel, despite the Genesis 2 principle, it was most common for a newlywed couple to live in close physical proximity to the man's family.

Yet despite the risks, leaving does not *require* physical separation from one's parents. Rather it points to a change in one's primary loyalty. A man's primary human loyalty is no longer to his parents but to his wife; likewise the woman's primary human loyalty shifts to her husband. When this loyalty shift has been firmly established and in-laws are helpful rather than intrusive or domineering, family nearness can be a blessing rather than a threat.

Question 6. Today in Western cultures many young couples assume they will share financial responsibilities; still, because of traditional expectations, the man may feel particularly insecure about his ability to provide for his wife. Especially if he gets married relatively young, he is likely still learning to handle many practical matters that his parents used to take care of. And if he does not yet fully trust the wisdom of his wife, he may tend to go to his parents for advice.

Question 7. Making sure that one's primary loyalty is to one's spouse builds trust and confidence in the new couple. Marriage is intended to be the most intimate relationship that human beings can enjoy. If there is a feeling that other relationships are more important, that intimate trust is threatened. Again, this does not mean that parents and others can't be consulted for their wisdom, but ultimately it is the new couple who makes final decisions together. Of course a young husband and wife are going to make some bad decisions that perhaps could have been avoided if their parents had gotten involved, but it can be healthy for a couple to struggle and learn on their own.

Question 8. Without question there are relationships, possessions and activities that can interfere with the development of a new primary loyalty between a husband and a wife. Some are particularly difficult for men to "leave"—for instance, friends. It is healthy to maintain friendships, and typically a husband's friends will have a good friendship with his wife as well. But no relationship should be more important than the relationship with one's wife.

Old habits may have to be left at the altar as well. It isn't that couples have to be just like each other, but a husband needs to stand ready to change annoying habits in order to spare the sanity of his wife.

Bonus. The language of Genesis 2 might lead one to conclude that married people are complete people while single people are desperately lonely people. But things are not quite that simple.

There *are* lonely single people who long for marriage but for various reasons have not found the right mate. Yet there are married people who are desperately lonely as well. (In a later study we will look at the reasons that marriage does not perfectly, or at times even start to, meet all our legitimate needs for companionship.)

Many single people are content without marriage. Paul recognizes and even encourages people who are contently single (1 Cor 7:8-9). Healthy friendships, an interesting career and an intimate relationship with God can lead to such contentment.

However, marriage *is* a significant means by which God addresses human loneliness. That it does not always lead to contentment is a function of human rebellion and sin.

Study 3. Leaving—from the Female Perspective. Psalm 45:10-15.

Purpose: To understand how a woman leaves her parents.

Question 1. Under normal circumstances a woman faces many challenges in a new marriage relationship. Her ties to home are strong. She is used to things being done a certain way in her old household, and now as a new primary loyalty is formed, patterns will change.

The woman described in Psalm 45 comes from Tyre, a city far away from Jerusalem, and she probably does not have much knowledge of the man she is marrying. Though in today's Western societies most brides know their groom better than she did, they still don't have a long track record with their husband that would give them confidence in his ability to care for them.

Question 2. Certainly she is not called to erase her memory of her childhood. To forget and remember are more than cognitive categories in the Old Testament. To remember someone is actually to obey them. So she is to forget her previous loyalty to her parents as she enters into this new relationship. Further, she isn't supposed to cultivate homesickness and pine away thinking about home.

Question 3. It may be difficult, but still it is fair. Indeed it is critical to the development of a strong marriage. If a woman is thinking constantly about her parents and what they would do and say, then her relationship with her new husband will be stifled. How difficult the transition is will depend in large part on the husband as well. A competent, responsible husband, like the one described in the first few verses of the psalm, helps diminish the insecurity of moving from one loyalty to another.

Question 4. Honoring one's husband would start with respect and admiration. It would involve a woman's putting her husband's interests ahead of her own. That does not mean she would always "obey" or fulfill his desires; his desires may not always conform to his best interest. To honor does not mean to be the servant of the husband.

Questions 5-6. An attitude of honor is still called for today—and such honoring is *not* only the wife's responsibility. A husband should respect and love his wife and put her best interest ahead of his own as well.

Question 7. For most people, leaving is a lifelong struggle. For one thing, old habits die hard. The pull of past patterns of behavior often keeps people from entering wholeheartedly into a new life with their spouse. This may manifest itself in subtle ways: for example, a wife expects her husband to be as competent in home repair as her father, or a husband demands that she mop the kitchen floor every evening just as his mother did. Or it can be more serious: a wife moves in with her mother whenever she has a fight with her husband.

Bonus. While in Genesis 2:24 the man is to leave his parents and in Psalm 45:10 the same call is extended to the woman, clearly parents themselves have a responsibility in the transition of their children from dependence to marriage independence. The parents have loved, helped and worried over their children from birth. Now, though they have entered a new relationship, there is a tendency to seek to continue the pattern. Married children may need to remind their parents that they need time alone and to assure them that they are doing well in navigating life.

Study 4. Weaving. Ecclesiastes 4:7-12.

Purpose: To explore the value of shared life and work with a marriage partner.

Question 1. After leaving his family of origin, the man is to "be joined" to his wife in anticipation of being united to her. *Joining* refers to all aspects of relationship that cause two people to become deeply involved in each other's life: spending time and having experiences together, speaking to each other, enjoying meals and praying together, and much, much more. Sexual intimacy is surely a large part of weaving a life together; it is given a special category in Genesis 2:24 in that it is specified by the third verb of the verse (being united or becoming one flesh). See study five.

Question 2. Work done in partnership is more productive, "more than" twice as much as solitary labor can yield. Further, another person will help you when you "fall." This is true literally but also figuratively. When one person fails at something or gets sick or has an accident, there is someone to provide strength in that moment of weakness. Verse 11 provides a touching picture of two people clinging together to share bodily warmth on a cold night. And a couple can protect each other during an assault. Thus Ecclesiastes 4 describes the advantages of *weaving* two lives into one. This can happen in a friendship and even more intensely in a marriage.

Question 3. Marriage is a more intense form of relationship than friendship; thus one can hope for even bigger dividends when spouses' lives are woven together. A spouse is physically and emotionally closer than a friend. A spouse is an intimate ally in the struggles of life. A wife is there is help a husband up when he falls. A husband is there to nurse his wife when she gets sick. At night they cuddle together for warmth and emotional support. They are there for each other in the midst of attack.

Question 4. Perhaps the single most important and difficult step toward weaving two lives into one is to create time to be together. It is important because there is no other way to really get to know each other than through being together, talking, sharing experiences. It is the most difficult because our twenty-first-century lives are crammed with all kinds of distractions, some urgent and necessary, some quite trivial. Concrete steps may include taking scheduled morning walks together or making sure you share certain mealtimes without interruption. The possibilities are endless, and both imagination and negotiation are needed for choosing and taking such steps.

Question 5. Among other reasons, shame and pride. We want to hide ourselves from others because we know we are inadequate and sinful. We don't want people to see our ugliness. We are also proud. We want to preserve our exalted position, and to share our hearts involves a vulnerability we are unwilling to grant.

The ability to open up our hearts to each other depends in large measure on whether we feel safe with our spouse. For this reason we need to be ready to extend grace to our spouse as they expose themselves to us. We also need to remember that our worth doesn't come from ourselves but from grace. We are sinners, but we are created in the image of God, and if we are Christians, our sin has been forgiven.

Question 6. Weaving our lives together shouldn't result in a union that eradicates differences. Each person brings his or her particular strengths and weaknesses to the relationship. A husband and a wife may have differing taste in movies, food, music; these differences can expand our horizons and spice up our lives.

Question 7. Each couple's relationship will take its own shape. Perhaps the spouses like different types of movies. One couple might agree to go together to see the favorite films of each. Another couple might decide that the husband will occasionally go with his friends to see the action movies the wife doesn't enjoy.

Question 8. Again, this will be a matter of negotiation. Whenever a wife or a husband feels threatened by the spouse's desire to keep a part of their life separate, it needs to be discussed and dealt with honestly and with a desire to preserve the relationship. Every relationship needs space, yet of all human relationships marriage is the most intimate. People may need time alone or time to be with friends, but with the blessing of their spouse.

Bonus. This type of love puts the other first, not oneself. It is tenacious in its hope for the future in spite of setbacks. It refuses to put up defenses; thus it is open to the other person. A key to weaving a life together is to refuse to close down to the other person. It also demands that we let our spouse know that we love them in spite of their inadequacies and struggles.

Study 5. Cleaving. Genesis 2:18-25.

Purpose: To see the place of sexual intimacy in marriage.

Question 1. God certainly knows that Adam is not going to find the companion to dispel his loneliness among the squirrels, chimps and meerkats. The review of all the animals helps Adam understand that they can't be adequate companions, that he needs more—and hence he is prepared to be amazed by the appearance of Eve.

Question 2. Eve's being created from Adam's body shows that the two began as one; they belong together and thus long for relationship. Note that Eve is created from the side or rib of Adam, not his head or his feet: she is his equal, not his subordinate nor his superior. They are partners, intimate allies.

Question 3. Many people have the mistaken view that the Bible *tolerates* sexual intercourse in marriage only because it is necessary to produce children. Yet here marriage is instituted without mention of children: this means that marriage and sexual relations have an even greater purpose than producing offspring. The pattern in Genesis 2 is "leave, weave and cleave," not "leave, weave, cleave and heave" in childbearing.

Question 4. There are no physical, emotional or spiritual barriers between Adam and Eve. They are not self-conscious of inadequacies; each is completely open to the other.

Question 5. God made us to enjoy certain bodily sensations, and sexual touch from someone we trust is highly stimulating.

Question 6. Sexual intimacy may only come after a new relationship is formed and the couple commit themselves to each other by breaking off old primary loyalties and joining their lives together emotionally and spiritually. Sex without that kind of commitment brings no more than momentary and superficial connection.

Question 7. As implied by the previous question, in and of itself, sex does not answer the question of loneliness. But sexual intimacy based on emotional and spiritual joining is a joyful and satisfying physical expression of oneness.

Bonus. Sex evokes tremendous desire because it is an intensely pleasurable physical experience. God built our bodies in such a way that we respond to seeing and being touched by another person. But sex is more than a physical experience. One sheds all cover, both physically and emotionally, in the act of sexual intercourse. There is no more intimate act than sex between a man and a woman. One reveals one's need for another and in a sense puts oneself at the mercy of the other, whose response can either affirm or crush. Thus sex can be a powerful means for enhancing a marriage relationship, but it can also threaten it.

Study 6. The Ultimate Loyalty. Psalm 127.

Purpose: To discover the importance of putting God at the center of your marriage.

Question 1. Of course "house" here is a metaphor for the family, just as "city" in the second half of the verse stands for a whole society. The principle is that strong family life and strong societies are formed when there is a strong relationship with God. The next psalm (128) pictures how the man who fears the Lord will have a flourishing family life with his wife and children.

Question 2. It is useless to try to build a strong marriage, family or society by our own strength. Our own resources are not adequate to the task. We will always fail if we try to do it ourselves. If we recognize that God is the foundation of a good relationship, then we can let go of our exhausting struggle to make things work.

Question 3. God should be the most important thing in our life. In the Garden of Eden, the perfect harmony that existed between Adam and Eve was possible because of their intimate relationship with God. Once the relationship with God was broken, Adam and Eve also became alienated from each other (Gen 3).

Question 4. To consider anything more important than God is to make it an idol. Whatever or whoever is most important to someone is their god, and anything or anyone other than the true God is a false god, an idol. Worship of an idol, even someone good like a spouse, is false worship. False gods will always disappoint us.

Question 5. To put a spouse ahead of God is to put a great burden on them. In essence they take the place of God, and expectations become unreasonably high. Being fallen and limited, an idolized spouse will always let you down. When a couple runs into difficulties that drain their resources, they have nowhere to turn if they haven't made God the most important thing in their life.

Question 6. An idol is anything or anyone that a person or a couple considers as more important than God. A couple can wrongly put money, social climbing, children or any number of things in that position.

Question 7. Together a husband and wife can decide to follow God by committing themselves to obey his will for their lives. They can make healthy commitments to seek God together in prayer, reading the Scriptures and joining a group of believers in whose company they can be accountable and learn. Through prayer they can bring their needs, questions and disagreements to God. Through the Scriptures they can get to know God better and learn what he desires.

Bonus. Psalm 127 encourages people to let the Lord build their house; in Matthew 7 Jesus' hearers are encouraged to build their house on the foundation of his teachings. A married couple should hear this as a call to reflect together on Jesus' teaching and obey it. In that way they can build a strong relationship.

While marriage is not specifically mentioned in 2 Corinthians 6, it is clear that Paul's warning applies to marriage. It would be hard to build a family on the foundation of the Lord if one partner is not committed to the Lord. It would be hard to build a house on the foundation of Jesus' teachings as instructed by Matthew 7:24-29 if one of the partners did not accept those teachings.

However, if someone is already married to an unbeliever, Paul elsewhere teaches that he or she should stay married with the hope that the spouse may be won to the Lord (1 Cor 7:12-16). Yet such a relationship will likely not be easy unless it stays at a very superficial level.